Withdrawn

NASCAR Tech

By Bob Woods

The Child's World

www.childsworld.com

www.childsworld.com

Published in the United States of America by
The Child's World®
1980 Lookout Drive • Mankato, MN 56003-1705
800-599-READ • www.childsworld.com

ACKNOWLEDGMENTS

The Child's World®:
Mary Berendes, Publishing Director

Produced by Shoreline Publishing Group LLC
President / Editorial Director: James Buckley, Jr.
Designer: Tom Carling, carlingdesign.com
Assistant Editor: Jim Gigliotti

Photo Credits:
Cover: AP/Wide World
Interior: AP/Wide World: 10, 15, 17, 21, 26;
Getty Images: 1, 4, 9, 16, 19, 22, 29; Reuters: 25;
Joe Robbins: 2, 7, 12, 23.

LIBRARY OF CONGRESS
CATALOGING-IN-PUBLICATION DATA

Woods, Bob.
  NASCAR tech / by Bob Woods.
      p. cm. — (The world of NASCAR)
  Includes bibliographical references and index.
  ISBN 978-1-60253-078-2 (library bound : alk.
paper)
  1. Stock car racing—United States—Juvenile
literature. 2.   Stock cars (Automobile)—United
States—Juvenile literature. 3.   NASCAR
(Association)—Juvenile literature. I. Title. II. Series.

  GV1029.9.S74W669 2008
  796.72--dc22

                  2007049079

Contents

[OPPOSITE]
*How do computers and technology help
get this awesome race car from the garage
to Victory Lane? Look inside!*

Welcome to the Future

WHEN WILLIAM "BIG BILL" FRANCE FOUNDED
the National Association for Stock Car Auto Racing—
NASCAR—in 1948, there was no such thing as a personal
computer. The Internet and cable television didn't exist.
That type of high technology was fantasized about in
science-fiction novels and movies.

The race cars and tracks were totally low-tech. Most
drivers showed up at unpaved, dirt ovals in souped-up
versions of the family sedans fans parked outside the
track. Drivers didn't have **crew chiefs**, teams of engineers
and mechanics, or **sponsors** paying for everything. The
action was fast, furious, and fun—but nothing fancy.

Fast-forward 60 years. NASCAR is now one of the
most popular spectator sports in the United States.
Millions of fans flock to hundreds of races held on
dozens of modern tracks across the country, or they
watch on TV. Fans also follow races on NASCAR.com.

Each driver's goal remains the same today as it
was in 1948: Go faster than everyone else and be the
first to cross the finish line when the **checkered flag** is
waved. Otherwise, NASCAR has gone through incredible
changes. Whether you look under the hood or down the
straightaway, technology is leading the way. Welcome
to the futuristic, high-tech world of NASCAR.

[OPPOSITE]
*In the old days, the
height of repair
work was a guy
straightening bent
metal with his hands.
NASCAR mechanics
have come a long way
since then.*

Here Today, Car of Tomorrow

IF DALE EARNHARDT JR.'S NO. 88 RACE CAR REALLY is a "**stock**" Chevrolet Impala SS, then the New York Yankees are just a bunch of Little Leaguers. Of course, neither is true. The Bronx Bombers and other Major League Baseball players are super-talented, professional athletes. Likewise, Junior's high-tech road rocket is hardly stock in the real meaning of the word. From their computer-designed bodies to their specially made tires, NASCAR racers are sophisticated, wondrous machines.

The original definition of a stock race car referred to a vehicle right out of the factory, with barely any changes made to it. But soon drivers modified, or changed the cars. The object was to make the cars go faster. Pretty soon, "stock" didn't accurately describe those race cars.

One reason why Bill France formed NASCAR in 1948 was to guarantee that all the "strictly stock" cars were similar. That way, races would be fair and competitive. The Fords, Chevys, Dodges, Hudsons, and early NASCAR racers were the same models average Americans drove.

Within a few years, though, car makers started replacing standard parts with ones that made the engine

All cars' colors are different, but their body style is the same. NASCAR teams all use the Car of Tomorrow.

more powerful and the **suspension** stronger. By the 1960s, developing new technology had become an important ingredient in stock car racing.

That trend has created fierce competition on and off the racetrack these days. A fearless, skilled driver will win more races if his race car is that much better than the other drivers' cars. That's why modern NASCAR Sprint Cup teams spend millions of dollars designing, building, testing, and preparing cars long before the track announcer says, "Gentlemen, start your engines!" Most every step of that road involves technology.

It's COT to Be Safe

Seven years of high-tech design and testing by NASCAR resulted in the Car of Tomorrow (COT). NASCAR's four car makers have their own versions, each hand-built by individual teams. Several features make the COT the safest stock car ever:

➤ The thick steel **roll cage** surrounding the driver has been enlarged.

➤ The driver's seat has been moved more toward the center of the protective cage.

➤ Steel plates added next to the doors protect the driver in a crash.

➤ **Aerodynamics** and handling are improved by adding a rear wing and a front "splitter" under the bumper. Both can be adjusted to conditions at different tracks.

NASCAR has strict rules requiring cars to have the same basic body and **chassis** design and similar engines. Minor adjustments are okay. Plenty of high-tech research and testing is allowed before and after races, however, which keeps teams extremely busy year round.

Building a stock car and getting it ready for race day is a complicated process. Long gone are those "strictly stock" days when **production models** zoomed around the track. Four major manufacturers—Chevy, Dodge, Ford, and Toyota—support NASCAR Sprint Cup teams. Their racers look similar to particular production models and their company logos remain on the cars. Other than that, there's barely any stock in these cars.

Lee Petty's Oldsmobile Super 88 car was not much different than the model fans could find at their local car dealership.

In 2007, NASCAR introduced the high-tech Car of Tomorrow (COT). It features general body, chassis, and engine designs that must be used by every driver in all Sprint Cup races. The car was built after seven years of hard work and lots of computer technology. The goal was to design a stock car that is safer, performs better, and is not as expensive as past models.

NASCAR's designers used special software programs to produce **three-dimensional** models of the COT. On the computer screen, the 3D models could be turned and viewed from any angle. That let designers test the car's aerodynamics (how air flows over the car at high speeds) and safety in a crash. Dozens of tests were first

Computer models helped NASCAR designers make the Car of Tomorrow safe and fast.

done on the computer before they built a real model and tested it on the track. The results were shared with every NASCAR driver's team. NASCAR teams use the information as a guide when they build their drivers' cars.

On days between races and during the off-season, NASCAR machines are put through a bunch of high-tech tests. For example, dozens of electronic **sensors** are wired up to different parts of the car. They transmit data to a computer while the car whips around the track. The sensors measure how the parts perform at high speeds. The information helps the team precisely "set up," or adjust, the car's engine and suspension for race day.

A car's aerodynamics also are tested in a wind tunnel. It's a large, enclosed space where high-speed fans blast wind at the front of a non-moving car. Sensors measure how the wind affects the car's front, sides, and rear. Workers can adjust parts of the car's body to improve its aerodynamics. The goal is to set up the car to go as fast as possible on race day without too much wind resistance, or **drag**. Making a race car today has come a long way from just going to car dealership and buying one!

The NASCAR Sprint Cup features versions of four popular production models:

➤ **Chevrolet Impala SS**
➤ **Dodge Avenger**
➤ **Ford Fusion**
➤ **Toyota Camry**

3

Technology Is a Team Effort

THE BRIGHTEST STARS IN NASCAR'S SPRINT CUP
races are the drivers. The daredevils behind the wheel definitely deserve the glory. Driving a 3,400-pound (1,542-kg) car with an 850-horsepower engine at speeds up to 200 miles (320 km) per hour is not easy. It takes years to gain the physical and mental skills necessary to reach NASCAR's top series. And what other job requires driving 500 miles on a Sunday afternoon?

There is not a single driver, however, who can succeed without a smart, hard-working team behind the scenes. The crew chief, mechanics, pit crew, and other team members may not get as much attention from fans and media. But the driver always gives them a high five when he wins a race. He knows that the checkered flag takes a total team effort.

Modern NASCAR teams run as smoothly as the fine-tuned engine under the hood of a high-tech stock car. Years ago, there were no teams. The driver himself did most of the work on the car in his garage at home. He'd round up a few friends or relatives for his pit crew on race days. As NASCAR grew, so too did the technology that went into the sport. By the 1980s, a driver needed a full-time team to stay competitive.

Today's teams are filled with college-educated designers, mechanics, and other technicians. "Just

[OPPOSITE]
Information from drivers like Matt Kenseth (right) joins data from computers to help team leaders make decisions.

about every job in NASCAR requires training," says John Dodson. He used to build stock cars for former NASCAR driver Rusty Wallace and now works at NASCAR's Technical Institute in Charlotte, North Carolina. "You can't just join a team right out of high school, as I did."

Taking NASCAR to School

Hollywood is home to the movie industry. New York City is the center of the financial world. And Charlotte, North Carolina, is the country's motor sports capital. Dozens of NASCAR teams and drivers call the Tar Heel State home, and most are located in and around Charlotte.

It's little surprise, then, that there are many colleges, universities, and technical schools in the Charlotte area where students can major in motorsports. Men and women take classes to become a designer, a mechanic, a crew chief, a pit crew member, a business manager, and other important jobs on a NASCAR team. With more and more demand for high-tech skills taught in these programs, motorsports grads have no trouble finding work.

Belmont Abbey College offers courses that teach the business side of motorsports. Students study sports **marketing**, racing management, and team management. The Motorsports Management program at Rowan-Cabarrus Community College covers everything from mechanics to marketing.

NASCAR Technical Institute is the only school in the country that can use the NASCAR name. "We're on the cutting edge of new technology," says John Dodson, who worked for many race teams before joining the school's staff. "NASCAR keeps us informed about changes in rules and technology."

Teams prefer to hire college graduates who have technical degrees and computer skills. In fact, several colleges and universities now offer courses that prepare students for jobs in racing. "Degrees are required to get the job I want in NASCAR," says Megan Montgomery, who studied mechanical engineering in college. She dreams of becoming a race-car designer.

Computers and other high-tech equipment is used by almost every member of a NASCAR team. The

Drivers and crew members need to get their heads into their work, sometimes peering deep inside engines to try to find a way to get a tiny bit more speed.

engines, **transmission**, brakes, and other parts of the race car are filled with dozens of electronic parts that mechanics need to know about. They analyze tons of data collected during a race. They use the data to make adjustments to the car for the next race.

During a race, the crew chief watches every lap from the team's spot on pit road. He has a computer that shows him not only how his driver is doing, but the other

Every team has a large cart with a platform on top. Crew members with computer monitors sit on the platform to help the driver run the best race he can.

Engineer-turned-racer Ryan Newman can "drive" a computer as well as his race car.

42 drivers in the race, too. He and the driver talk to each other over a special two-way radio throughout the race. The crew chief tells the driver things like when to pass or when someone's going to pass him. The computer reports exactly how much gas the car has used, so the crew chief also tells the driver when to make a pit stop for more fuel and to replace worn-out tires.

Even some drivers are going high-tech. Ryan Newman, the NASCAR Cup Series Rookie of the Year in 2002, graduated from Purdue University in 2001 with a degree in "vehicle structure engineering," which means how cars are put together. His college education gives him a great understanding of how his high-tech No. 12 race car works. It also helps him communicate with his crew chief, race engineer, and other crew members who also have engineering degrees. "We have a common language and background to work with in trying to make the race car fast," Ryan says. Now, that's smart teamwork.

In early 2008, Newman was quoted as saying that he wished he was not alone as a college graduate driving in NASCAR. "I wish more kids said, 'I want to get an education and then go to NASCAR.'"

4

Space-Age Racetracks

AT FIRST GLANCE, A PAVED RACETRACK MIGHT not appear to be abuzz with high technology. Above and below the surface of 21st-century speedways where NASCAR races are held, however, many technological wonders can be discovered. From digital timing and scoring systems to foam-padded steel walls, today's tracks are smarter and safer than ever.

Just as race cars have come a long way since the "strictly stock" days, so have the tracks they speed around. NASCAR's very first race in 1949, was run on a 0.75-mile (1.2-km) dirt track in Charlotte, North Carolina. A crowd of nearly 13,000 cheered as the cars kicked up dust sometimes so thick, fans couldn't see the action.

The following year, the sport's first paved track opened in Darlington, South Carolina. A crowded field of 75 cars entered the Southern 500. The drivers welcomed the chance to test their skills on the smooth, 1.25-mile (2-km) track. The cars certainly went faster on asphalt than on dirt, but the greater speeds wore down tires much quicker. That meant more pit stops to replace tires. The winner, Johnny Mantz, wisely decided to put heavier truck tires on his racer.

Gradually, the short, dirt tracks were replaced by longer, paved ones. By 2008, NASCAR's 36 Sprint Cup

No soft walls, no smooth asphalt, no protective screens—dirt tracks like these were the home of NASCAR in the early days.

SAFER Racetracks

At the start of a NASCAR race, a track official waves a green flag. At the end, a black-and-white checkered flag waves, first as the winner and then every other car crosses the finish line. And there's the yellow flag. It signals caution, usually following a crash, and the cars must slow down.

Most NASCAR races feature several yellow flags. Unfortunately, crashes are a fact of life in stock car racing. Fortunately, drivers suffer very few serious injuries. Years of high-tech research and development have led to the extremely safe Car of Tomorrow. Track safety has greatly improved, too,

One major area of concern are the concrete walls that surround racetracks. There's no way to avoid cars occasionally crashing into them, but now NASCAR has made those accidents less dangerous. With the help of researchers at the famous Indianapolis Motor Speedway, NASCAR used computer models to test what happens when a car crashes into a wall at high speeds. Using the data, they produced what's called the SAFER barrier.

SAFER stands for Steel and Foam Energy Reduction. The barrier, about 30 inches thick, is a combination of steel tubes and thick foam blocks that soften the impact when a car hits it. Imagine having a giant mattress to break your fall onto a concrete floor. SAFER barriers have been installed in front of existing walls at most every NASCAR racetrack. So far, they're a big hit with safety-minded drivers.

races were run on 22 different tracks. Lengths vary from the .526-mile (.8-km) short track in Martinsville, Virginia, to the 2.66-mile (4.3-km) superspeedway in Talladega, Alabama. Most are oval-shaped tracks, where cars race counterclockwise and make only left-hand turns. Two tracks, Infineon in California and Watkins Glen in New York, are twisty road courses with right and left turns.

Regardless, every Cup Series track is ultra-modern. Daytona International Speedway, in Daytona Beach, Florida, is a great example. The home of the famous Daytona 500 opened in 1959. The track is 2.5 miles (4 km) long and seats 168,000 fans. They enjoy the live sights and sounds of 43 cars roaring around the track. Fans also can follow the race on a gigantic video screen

Here's a good look at a SAFER wall. You can see the foam blocks that would cushion a car during a crash.

or rent headsets and listen to the track announcers. The latest gadget is FanView, a hand-held device that fans at the track can buy or rent. It carries live video and audio of the race and in-car camera views from seven drivers.

Amazing technology that fans won't see are the dozens of electronic sensors buried around the track. Nor will anyone see each car's **transponder**, a small device that sends an electronic signal which is received by the sensors. The two-way system allows NASCAR officials to electronically follow the cars around the racetrack.

Drivers and crew members use radio technology to speak to each other. They also use radios to do media interviews. Here, driver Greg Biffle checks in with his crew after a practice lap.

The yellow bump shown on top of Matt Kenseth's car contains the transponder.

The digital information gathered during every lap is called "loop data," which is saved in computers. The data pinpoints every car's position and speed throughout the race. It also records whenever cars pass each other and their speed through turns. That fancy system has created many new statistics that teams and fans use to analyze a race. Among the stats are "quality passes," "speed in traffic," and "consecutive passes."

Perhaps most important, the data is used to decide the winner of a race too close to call with the naked eye or even with close-up photographs. With loop data, a finish can be measured in fractions of a second. That blink of an eye can be the difference between first and second place. So thanks to space-age technology, there's never any doubt about which driver takes that good, old-fashioned checkered flag.

How close is "close"? The closest finish in NASCAR history came in a 2003 race at Darlington, South Carolina. Ricky Craven beat Kurt Busch by .002 seconds. That's less than the time it takes to blink your eye!

5

The Digital NASCAR Fan

THERE'S NOTHING QUITE LIKE BEING AT A NASCAR race in person. Sitting in the grandstands with thousands of other fans, cheering for your favorite driver, is a huge thrill. These days, however, watching a race from the comfort of your home is a whole different experience. NASCAR has added so many high-tech goodies, it's almost like riding right in the car with that favorite driver.

Television has played a starring role in NASCAR's rise in popularity. Today, every lap of every Sprint Cup race is broadcast live on national TV. That wasn't always the case, however.

Sports television dates back to 1939, when a college baseball game aired on NBC. By the 1960s, baseball, football, and basketball were TV regulars. The 1979 Daytona 500 was the first NASCAR race telecast from start to finish. After that, more and more races were shown on television. Now NASCAR is all over network, cable, and pay TV, as well as the Internet. In fact, NASCAR is the No. 2 sport on television after National Football League broadcasts.

No sport, however, brings the fan closer to the action than NASCAR. It's always adding new technology to make each race more exciting. Twenty years ago, a network covered a race with just a few TV cameras, a couple of

Look out behind you! No, these fans aren't being run over—they're standing in front of a huge TV screen. It lets fans at the race see what fans at home see.

NASCAR crew members use video feeds to watch their driver in action or to watch other drivers. Of course, they can also take a break during a practice session to check on a football game, too!

broadcasters in the booth, and a handful of reporters talking to the drivers and crews in the pits.

These days, Fox Sports is one of several networks that take turns covering NASCAR during the season. Fox uses 18 manned cameras, two super-slow-motion cameras, 10 **robotic** cameras, 14 in-car sets of three cameras each, and at least 150 microphones. ESPN has mini-cameras attached to pit-crew members' helmets and planted in the grass around the track. And don't forget eye-in-the-sky blimp cameras.

The networks have teams of announcers in the booth, the pits, and all around the track. Dozens of directors, camera operators, researchers, editors, and technicians work behind the scenes. Most of the races are broadcast in high-definition.

Other TV wizardry includes 3D animated images of cars in real-time. "Draft Track" is a special effect that shows viewers how air flows over and behind race cars. The technology is similar to that used to show the line of scrimmage and first-down line during NFL games on TV.

Live from the Racetrack

Every week during the NASCAR Sprint Cup season, from February to November, TV crews travel across the country to broadcast another race. Each one is a gigantic production that involves a small army of hardworking people, tons of high-tech equipment, and millions of fans enjoying the broadcast at home.

A typical week begins right after one race wraps up and the crew begins preparing for the next one. The equipment—including about 80 cameras, 30 videotape machines, several dozen video monitors, 150 microphones, a maze of antennas and **satellite** dishes, and more than 100,000 feet of fiber-optic cable—is packed into as many as 18 tractor-trailers. Part of the typical 160-person crew travels with the caravan of trucks, called haulers. Others fly to their next destination.

In football terms, the producer is the head coach. He or she does the planning for each race. The director is the quarterback, who makes sure everyone does their jobs on race day. On the days before the race, the producer and director meet with the crew. They discuss unique things about broadcasting from that track. They decide which drivers to interview and what interesting stories to tell viewers.

In 2007, DirecTV, the satellite TV service, introduced "HotPass." This special coverage, separate from what the networks show on "free" TV, costs DirecTV subscribers about $100 for the season. Each week, HotPass teams up with five different drivers. Each driver has his own DirecTV channel, with an announcer and a pit reporter. Viewers can flip to any of the five channels and watch live video from inside the car and the pits. They also can listen to live radio chatter between the driver and his crew chief.

Satellite Radio has NASCAR covered, too. Subscribers can switch back and forth among 10 audio channels, each one following a different driver. Listeners can hear drivers talking to their teams and tune into the official radio broadcast of the race.

NASCAR.com, the sport's official Web site, provides an amazing variety of online options for fans who like to follow Sprint Cup races on their computers. They can subscribe to TrackPass and get exclusive access to three live, in-race features. 1) RaceView shows each car in 3D, similar to a video game. While watching and listening to the race, fans get pit stats, crash and caution updates, and lap-by-lap commentary. 2) PitCommand uses GPS (global positioning system) technology to follow each car as it circles the track. Options include real-time animation of drivers' speedometers, in-car communications between

Satellite radio is different than regular radio. With regular radio, the signals can be heard with normal radios (in cars, in homes, etc.) With satellite radio, however, people need special receivers tuned to satellites in outer space.

drivers and pit crews, and the radio broadcast of the race. 3) Scanner allows fans to listen to each team's audio communications during the race.

Fans use technology to enjoy NASCAR off the track, too! Video games that let you be part of the action are very popular.

There's one thing to keep in mind about NASCAR and technology. Both are only going to keep growing and improving, year after year. By the time NASCAR reaches its 100th anniversary—in 2048—there's no telling what high-tech wonders race cars, drivers, teams, tracks, and fans will enjoy. It's sure to be a wild ride.

Glossary

aerodynamics   the study of how air flows around an object

chassis   the steel frame or skeleton of a car

checkered flag   a black-and-white flag waved to end a race

crew chief   the person in charge of a NASCAR race team

drag   wind or air resistance

marketing   telling people about a product or service

production models   cars produced for the public to drive

robotic   controlled by electronics

roll cage   a steel cage around the driver of a race car

satellite   a machine that orbits the Earth

sensors   small electronic parts that send information to a computer

sponsors   companies that pay athletes to promote their products or services

stock   original from the factory

straightaway   the long, straight sections of racetracks located between the curved corners

suspension   the parts of a car that help it stay balanced and smooth while moving

three-dimensional   having the appearance of height, width, and depth

transmission   the parts of a car that help it switch gears

transponder   a part of a car that sends back signals to a computer during a race

Find Out More

BOOKS

Eyewitness NASCAR
By James Buckley, Jr.
DK Publishing, 2005
A photo-filled look at everything about NASCAR from the tires on up. Technology sections include a look inside the car, information about engine design, and pit-crew training.

NASCAR Designed to Win
By Mike Kennedy and Mark Stewart
Lerner Books, 2007
Visit NASCAR team garages and meet the experts who give NASCAR drivers the cars and engines they need to win.

Pit Pass
By Bob Woods
Readers' Digest Children's Publishing, 2005
An inside look at every part of NASCAR racing, from how pit crews do their job to how a race is run. Meet top drivers, learn more "tech talk," and find out more about how NASCAR started.

Stock Car Secrets
By Jim Francis
Crabtree Publishing, 2008
From the headlight stickers to the aerodynamic rear spoiler, take a bolt-by-bolt look at how a NASCAR vehicle goes from a designer's mind to the racetrack.

WEB SITES

Visit our Web site for lots of links about NASCAR technology:
www.childsworld.com/links

Note to Parents, Teachers, and Librarians: We routinely check our Web links to make sure they're safe, active sites—so encourage your readers to check them out!

Index

ABOUT THE AUTHOR

Bob Woods is a writer who lives in Connecticut. He has written many books and magazine articles about motor sports, and was the editor of the Harley-Davidson motorcycle company's 100th anniversary magazine.